LUCERNE

TRAVEL GUIDE

2023

"Discover the Enchanting Beauty of
Lucerne: A Comprehensive Travel Guide"

KYLE WATSON

Table of content

INTRODUCTION
    About Lucerne
    Why Visit Lucerne
    Getting to Lucerne
    Essential Travel Information
EXPLORING LUCERNE'S HISTORIC CHARM
NATURAL BEAUTY AND OUTDOOR ADVENTURES
CULTURAL DELIGHTS IN LUCERNE
LUCERNE'S GASTRONOMY AND CULINARY SCENE
DAY TRIPS FROM LUCERNE
FESTIVALS AND EVENTS IN LUCERNE
    Lucerne Festival: A Celebration of Classical Music
    Fasnacht Lucerne: Carnival Extravaganza
    Blue Balls Festival: Music and Arts on the Lake
    Lucerne Christmas Market: Magical Holiday Spirit
PRACTICAL INFORMATION FOR TRAVELERS
    Accommodation Options: Hotels, Hostels, and More
    Transportation within Lucerne: Buses, Trains, and Boats
    Important Travel Advice and Safety Advice
    Shopping in Lucerne: Souvenirs and Local Products
    Lucerne Travel Itineraries
CONCLUSION
    Final Thoughts on Lucerne

Planning Your Perfect Trip to Lucerne
Useful Resources and Contacts

INTRODUCTION

About Lucerne

The gorgeous city of Lucerne, sometimes known as the "Gem of Switzerland," is located in Central Switzerland. Lucerne, which is situated on the shores of Lake Lucerne and surrounded by breathtaking alpine scenery, is well known for its alluring beauty and extensive cultural history.

With a history that stretches back to the eighth century, the city has long been a center for commerce and tourism. With its picturesque cobblestone walkways, vibrant facades, and historical buildings, Lucerne's Old Town transports tourists to a bygone period.

Lucerne, which has 80,000 people, provides a lovely combination of traditional charm and contemporary refinement. It acts as a hub for culture, holding several annual festivals, concerts, and events. Lucerne is a well-liked resort for outdoor lovers and adventure seekers since it serves as a gateway to the Swiss Alps.

Travelers of all interests are guaranteed a thrilling and wonderful experience in Lucerne, whether they want to walk along the famous Chapel Bridge, visit world-class museums, take a boat tour on Lake Lucerne, or immerse themselves in the local culinary scene.

We will explore the different sights, things to do, and cultural treats that Lucerne has to offer in this thorough travel guide. This guide will provide you with all the knowledge you need to make the most of your trip to Lucerne in 2023, from historical sites to natural marvels, gastronomic pleasures to yearly celebrations. Let's go off on a tour to explore Lucerne's alluring charm!

Why Visit Lucerne

There are several compelling reasons to go to Lucerne. Here are a few:

Beautiful Natural Setting: Lucerne is endowed with beautiful natural surroundings. The breathtaking alpine scenery, immaculate lakes, and towering mountains that make Lucerne a sanctuary for nature lovers may be experienced in full in 2023. The natural splendor of Lucerne will wow you whether you're climbing Mount Pilatus, sailing on Lake Lucerne, or seeing the lovely Swiss countryside.

Rich Cultural Legacy: The well-preserved architecture, historic sites, and cultural institutions of Lucerne are tangible examples of the city's rich history and cultural legacy. In 2023, you may explore the historic Musegg Wall, marvel at the famed Lion Monument, and visit the renowned Chapel Bridge to learn more about Lucerne's history. World-class museums and galleries that highlight the contributions of the city's culture are also found in Lucerne.

Bright Festivals and Events: Throughout the year, Lucerne hosts several bright festivals and events that are well-known. You may attend the famous Lucerne Festival in 2023, a festival of classical music including performers that are well-known across the world. Take part in the vibrant and vivacious Fasnacht Lucerne, a carnival spectacle, or attend the Blue Balls Festival to immerse yourself in the arts. These activities give amazing enjoyment and a special look into the local culture.

Outdoor Adventures: Lucerne is the perfect place for adventure seekers. You may start engaging in exhilarating outdoor pursuits like hiking, skiing, snowboarding, and paragliding in 2023. You can explore the spectacular mountain peaks, take on strenuous hikes, and take in the natural beauty of the Swiss Alps with ease. There are several options for heart-pounding thrills in Lucerne.

Gastronomic Delights: Foodies will delight in Lucerne's gastronomic scene. In 2023, you may relish authentic Swiss gastronomy, indulge in premium cheeses and chocolates, and visit bustling food markets. Lucerne provides a wide variety of gastronomic experiences that will excite your taste buds, from warm local pubs to Michelin-starred restaurants.

Warm Swiss Hospitality: Lucerne residents are renowned for their warm friendliness and outgoing personalities. You may enjoy the warm ambiance and sincere welcome that make Lucerne a wonderful destination in 2023. The locals are always willing to share their experiences, suggest undiscovered attractions, and make your stay special.

You will get a one-of-a-kind chance to see Lucerne's natural beauty, learn about its fascinating history, and take part in exhilarating festivals and activities in 2023 when you go there. Lucerne guarantees an exceptional holiday experience that will leave you with treasured memories for years to come thanks to its friendly friendliness and variety of activities.

Getting to Lucerne

In the center of Switzerland, Lucerne is readily accessible by a variety of means of transportation. The following are the primary ways to go to Lucerne:

By Air: Zurich Airport (ZRH), located around 65 kilometers (40 miles) from Lucerne, is the nearest major airport. You may use a train, a cab, or a vehicle to get to

Lucerne from Zurich Airport. There are several direct connections available and the train ride lasts around an hour. The other option is to take a cab or rent a vehicle at the airport and go by road to Lucerne.

By Train: Switzerland boasts a first-rate rail system, and Lucerne is well-connected to the country's main cities and villages. Taking a train to Lucerne is a practical alternative if you're coming from Switzerland or one of its nearby nations, like Germany or Italy. Regular rail service from several locations is provided to Lucerne by the Swiss Federal Railways (SBB). Lucerne's railway station is well situated, making it simple to get to various areas of the city.

By automobile: Lucerne is readily accessible by automobile and has good access to Switzerland's main thoroughfares. Depending on traffic, it takes 45 minutes or less to drive from Zurich to Lucerne on the A4/E41 expressway. It's crucial to remember that parking in the city center may be difficult and costly, so it's best to plan or utilize public transit to navigate about Lucerne.

By Bus: Both domestic and foreign bus routes run in Lucerne. You may search for direct bus routes to Lucerne from your location if you want to take a bus. Buses are a cheap alternative that can provide beautiful views of the Swiss landscape.

By Boat: Traveling by boat is another unusual method to get to Lucerne. There are boat services that link the numerous cities and villages surrounding Lake Lucerne, which is navigable. If you are traveling from one of the lakeside cities, you may take a leisurely boat journey to Lucerne while admiring the stunning scenery en route.

Once you get there, Lucerne is a somewhat small city that is simple to get about on foot. Navigating the city and getting to its attractions and neighboring regions is simple thanks to Lucerne's effective public transit system, which includes buses and trams.

Getting to Lucerne is easy, and the trip there may be picturesque and delightful regardless of your mode of transportation of choice—air, rail, car, bus, or boat.

Essential Travel Information

To guarantee a smooth and pleasurable vacation, it's vital to acquire some crucial travel information before visiting Lucerne. Here are some important things to think about:

Visa Requirements: Since Switzerland is a member of the Schengen Area, tourists from several nations do not need a visa for brief visits of up to 90 days. Checking the visa requirements depending on your nationality and the reason for your travel is crucial, nevertheless. Ensure your passport is valid for at least six more months than the length of time you want to remain.

Currency: The Swiss Franc (CHF) is the currency used in Lucerne and across Switzerland. It's a good idea to check the conversion rates before your travel and to bring enough cash with you for quick purchases. Although most hotels, restaurants, and stores take credit cards, it's a good idea to have extra cash on hand just in case.

Language: German, French, and Italian are Lucerne's official languages. However, many people speak English, particularly in tourist hotspots. Although you won't often have any problem talking in English, it never hurts to learn a few fundamental words and phrases in the local tongue.

Weather and Packing: The climate in Lucerne is moderate, with four different seasons. Winters (December to February) may be cold and snowy, but summers (June to August) are often pleasant to warm. Before your journey, it's crucial to check the weather prediction and prepare appropriately. Bring any specialized gear you'll need for outdoor sports or trips, as well as comfortable walking shoes, layers of clothes, a waterproof jacket, and other necessary goods.

Travel insurance: Having travel insurance that pays for medical costs, trip cancellation, and lost or stolen possessions is strongly advised. To be sure you have enough coverage for your trip to Lucerne, check with your insurance company.

Health and Safety: Although Lucerne is a safe city for visitors, it's still crucial to practice standard safety measures. Be aware of your possessions and refrain from leaving valuables unattended. Although Switzerland has excellent medical facilities, it is still a good idea to obtain travel insurance that includes medical emergencies. Make sure to carry enough medicine with you if you need to take any special drugs.

Local Customs and Etiquette: It's beneficial to be informed of Switzerland's specific customs and etiquette while you're there. Although not required, tips are welcomed for excellent service. It's customary to shake hands while greeting someone and use formal titles unless first names are requested. Due to the great significance placed on timeliness in Switzerland, it is advised to be on time for appointments and trips.

Electricity: Switzerland utilizes 230V plugs that are Type C and Type J standard across Europe. You may need a travel adapter or voltage converter if your nation has a different plug type or voltage.

The majority of Lucerne's hotels, eateries, and public areas have Wi-Fi connections. For continuous internet access throughout your visit, you may also acquire SIM cards or mobile data subscriptions from regional service providers.

Before your journey to Lucerne, it is essential to verify the most recent travel warnings and recommendations from the embassy or consulate of your country. You can guarantee a trouble-free and enjoyable visit to this charming Swiss city by being well-prepared and educated.

EXPLORING LUCERNE'S HISTORIC CHARM

The best way to appreciate Lucerne's ancient appeal is to explore its preserved monuments, cobblestone streets, and intriguing historical tales. We shall examine some of the well-known landmarks that highlight Lucerne's lengthy history in this part.

Old Town: A Walkthrough of Lucerne's Historic Center

Enter the Old Town of Lucerne to go back in time. A compelling ambiance is created by the well-preserved medieval buildings, the little lanes, and the vibrant façade. Take a leisurely walk through the pedestrian-only streets to see gorgeous squares, beautiful fountains, and welcoming stores.

The Weinmarkt Square, the center of the Old Town, with its Renaissance-style structures and stunning Rathaus (Town Hall), should not be missed as you explore. You may locate the Altes Kaufhaus (Old Market Hall), a remarkable structure that was once a hub for commerce, on the Kornmarkt Square if you keep walking.

Chapel Bridge and Water Tower: Iconic Symbols of Lucerne

The Chapel Bridge (Kapellbrücke), a covered wooden bridge that crosses the Reuss River, is one of Lucerne's most well-known sights. The oldest covered wooden bridge in Europe was constructed in the 14th century, and it serves as the city's emblem. Admire the paintings from the 17th century that illustrate events from Lucerne's past as you stroll around the bridge.

The round stone Water Tower (Wasserturm), which was once a defense tower and is now a jail, is located in the center of Chapel Bridge. For sweeping views of the city and its surroundings, climb the tower. A recognizable picture of Lucerne is often connected with the Chapel Bridge and Water Tower together.

Musegg Wall: Discovering Lucerne's Medieval Fortifications

An interesting example of Lucerne's medieval defenses is the Musegg Wall. Four of the nine towers of this well-preserved city wall, which dates to the fourteenth century, are accessible to the public. Enjoy sweeping views of the city, Lake Lucerne, and the surrounding Alps by strolling along the wall.

One of the Musegg Wall's most noticeable towers is the Zyt Tower. It contains the Zytglogge, Lucerne's oldest clock, which chimes every hour. Don't pass up the chance to see this mechanical wonder and take in the clock tower's heritage.

Lion Monument: A Tribute to Swiss Guards

A striking and moving artwork, the Lion Monument (Löwendenkmal), honors the Swiss Guards who perished during the French Revolution. The monument, which was carved into a rock face, shows a dying lion laying his paw on a shield with the fleur-de-lis of the French dynasty. This famous structure stands as a testament to bravery, devotion, and selflessness.

The Lion Monument is a stirring attraction, and the quiet environment of the little park where it is located adds to the mood of reflection. Consider for a minute the craftsmanship and value of this monument.

You may immerse yourself in the enchanting history of Lucerne by exploring the city's historic charm. Visitors are left with a lasting image of Lucerne's rich legacy as they stroll through the charming Old Town, over the famous Chapel Bridge, explore the ancient defenses of the Musegg Wall, and pay homage at the Lion Monument.

NATURAL BEAUTY AND OUTDOOR ADVENTURES

Lucerne is endowed with a wealth of natural beauty, providing tourists with a diverse selection of outdoor activities and picturesque landscapes to discover. Nature lovers and adventure seekers will find enough to enjoy, from the serene waters of Lake Lucerne to the spectacular summits of Mount Pilatus, Rigi, and Engelberg-Titlis. Let's explore the natural splendors that Lucerne has to offer.

Lake Lucerne: Sailing, Cruising, and Watersports

The gorgeous Lake Lucerne, sometimes referred to as the "Lake of the Four Forested Cantons," is encircled by beautiful mountains. For those who like the water, this large lake provides a wide variety of activities. Take a leisurely boat ride and

22

enjoy the stunning sights of the area's scenery. A lot of cruises provide narrations in many languages that share intriguing information and anecdotes about the area.

Sailing, paddleboarding, or kayaking are other watersports that are suitable for individuals looking for a more energetic experience. On warm days, a relaxing dip in Lake Lucerne's crystal-clear waters is the ideal way to cool down. To try your luck at capturing native fish species, you may also rent a boat or go on a fishing tour.

Mount Pilatus: A Majestic Mountain Escape

Mount Pilatus, which rises sharply on the outskirts of Lucerne, provides a spectacular mountain retreat with panoramic views and thrilling activities. You may ride the world's steepest cogwheel train for scenery to get to the peak. Admire the breathtaking views of the surroundings as you rise.

You'll be rewarded at the summit with stunning views of the Swiss Alps and Lake Lucerne. Discover the network of hiking routes that are suitable for all skill levels and immerse yourself in the splendor of the mountains. Instead, take advantage of the chance to attempt paragliding for a bird's-eye perspective of the area.

Mount Pilatus has food choices, a tourist center, and the option to spend the night at the Pilatus Kulm Hotel in addition to outdoor activities. Experiences of the sun setting and rising atop the mountain are especially unforgettable because the sky's shifting hues give a wonderful radiance over the surroundings.

Rigi: The Queen of Mountains

Rigi, often known as the "Queen of Mountains," is a stunning natural landmark close to Lucerne that draws tourists with its breathtaking scenery. Rigi, which is accessible by a charming cogwheel train or cable car, has sweeping views of Lake Lucerne and the nearby Alps.

Explore the well-designated hiking routes that go through beautiful meadows and woodlands after you've reached the peak. For lovers of nature, it is a paradise because of the variety of flora and wildlife. For those wanting an adrenaline rush on two wheels, Rigi also has a network of mountain bike tracks.

Take a stop at one of the little mountain eateries and indulge in authentic Swiss cuisine while taking in the breathtaking views. In Rigi, you can see the sunset, which illuminates the surrounding area with a golden light as it descends over the horizon.

Engelberg-Titlis: Alpine Adventures and Skiing

Travelers seeking winter sports and alpine thrills must make the trek to Engelberg-Titlis. Engelberg-Titlis, which is close to Lucerne, provides a wide range of outdoor activities all year round.

Skiers and snowboarders from all over the globe go to the area during the winter months when it changes into a snowy paradise. The Mount Titlis slopes provide a variety of pistes and off-piste chances to accommodate skiers of all skill levels. Even during the summer, skiers and snowboarders may use the Titlis Glacier.

Numerous other activities are available in Engelberg-Titlis in addition to winter sports. Ride a cable car to Mount Titlis' peak to enjoy the breathtaking Ice Flyer chairlift, which offers sweeping views of the region's glaciers. Visit the Glacier Cave to see the intriguing subterranean world filled with ice formations and sculptures.

Mountain bikers and hikers will find Engelberg-Titlis to be a wonderland in the summer. Discover the network of hiking routes that take you to beautiful valleys, alpine lakes, and spectacular vistas. Mountain bikers may take advantage of exhilarating downhill routes or set out on beautiful rides through the Swiss countryside.

A well-liked location for climbing and mountaineering is Engelberg-Titlis. While novice climbers may join guided climbing tours or via Ferrata routes, where iron rungs and cables aid in the ascent, experienced climbers can attempt the difficult summits.

After a day of outdoor exploration, relax in Engelberg, a quaint Swiss town renowned for its warmth and inviting ambiance. Experience the alpine beauty of the area while sampling regional cuisine at the restaurants and cafés.

There are several options to get in touch with nature and partake in exhilarating activities thanks to Lucerne's scenic surroundings and outdoor activities. You're certain to make priceless memories among Switzerland's breathtaking scenery, whether you're boating on Lake Lucerne, climbing Mount Pilatus and Rigi, or enjoying alpine activities in Engelberg-Titlis.

CULTURAL DELIGHTS IN LUCERNE

Lucerne is recognized for its thriving cultural life in addition to its stunning natural scenery. The city provides a multitude of cultural pleasures that appeal to all creative preferences, from top-notch music venues to interesting museums. Take advantage of Lucerne's rich cultural offerings by visiting the following places:

Lucerne Culture and Congress Center

On the shores of Lake Lucerne sits a marvel of architecture called the Lucerne Culture and Congress Center, or KKL Luzern. This cutting-edge cultural complex, created by famous French architect Jean Nouvel, serves as a focal point for concerts, exhibitions, and music.

The Lucerne Symphony Orchestra resides in the facility, which also presents a range of events featuring jazz, classical, and modern music. The concert hall's outstanding acoustics provide a captivating and unforgettable musical experience.

The KKL Luzern presents visual arts, dance performances, theatrical shows, and movie screenings in addition to music. Investigate the center's display areas to find a wide variety of creative expressions.

Richard Wagner Museum

A trip to the Richard Wagner Museum is essential for opera aficionados and Richard Wagner admirers. Wagner resided at the Tribschen villa from 1866 until 1872, and the museum there provides a special look into his life and compositions.

You'll come across authentic antiques, Wagner-related papers, personal items, and musical instruments as you explore the museum. Learn more about his creative process and the impact he had on the operatic world.

The museum has breathtaking views of Lake Lucerne and is surrounded by lovely gardens. Take time to enjoy the serene setting that previously served as Wagner's source of inspiration.

Swiss Museum of Transport

Visit the Swiss Museum of Transport (Verkehrshaus der Schweiz) to explore the amazing world of transportation. This interactive museum, which is close to Lucerne, illustrates the development of transportation in Switzerland and beyond.

Learn about the technical developments that have influenced the way we travel as you peruse the sizable collection of historic automobiles, trains, ships, and other transportation. Visitors of all ages will find the museum to be interesting and informative thanks to the interactive exhibits, simulators, and multimedia displays.

The Hans Erni Museum, which showcases the creations of famous Swiss artist Hans Erni, is also housed inside the Swiss Museum of Transport. Admire his stunning paintings, sculptures, and murals, many of which feature the beauty of Switzerland and transportation-related subjects.

The Rosengart Collection: Art from Picasso to Klee

The Rosengart Collection, a vast collection of contemporary art, will thrill art lovers. The museum, which is housed in a gorgeously renovated building in Lucerne's Old Town, is home to an exceptional collection of 19th- and 20th-century works of art.

The collection includes pieces by well-known painters such as Marc Chagall, Paul Klee, Claude Monet, and Pablo Picasso. Admire the magnificent Cubist works of Picasso, delve into the vibrant and innovative compositions of Klee, and learn about the many artistic trends represented in the collection.

You have a one-of-a-kind chance to immerse yourself in the world of contemporary art at the museum and learn about the creative vision and methods of some of the finest 20th-century painters.

Explore Lucerne's thriving art scene and immerse yourself in its many cultural offerings. These cultural destinations, ranging from the cutting-edge KKL Luzern to the Richard Wagner Museum, the Swiss Museum of Transport, and the Rosengart Collection, provide an enthralling trip through music, art, and history. Discover

Lucerne's rich cultural legacy, and let it inspire and enhance your trip.

LUCERNE'S GASTRONOMY AND CULINARY SCENE

For food lovers, Lucerne is not only a visual feast but also a gastronomic treat. The culinary sector of the city has a variety of mouthwatering cuisine, regional delicacies, and luxurious desserts. Explore the following facets of Lucerne's cuisine and culinary scene as you go on a gastronomic journey:

Traditional Swiss Cuisine: Must-Try Dishes

Don't pass up the chance to sample authentic Swiss food when visiting Lucerne. Among the meals you must try are:

Fondue: Cheese fondue is a specialty of Switzerland, and Lucerne is no exception. Dip slices of bread into a saucepan of melted

Swiss cheese, which is often seasoned with white wine and garlic. It's a convivial and cozy dining experience.

Raclette: This delicious cheese-based dish calls for melted cheese to be scraped from cooked potatoes, pickles, and onions. A rich and delicious dinner is enhanced by the creamy and tasty topping made from melted cheese.

Rösti: A popular meal in Switzerland, rösti is a main course or side of fried potatoes. In addition to being often served with meat, cheese, or eggs, grated potatoes are pan-fried till golden brown. It is considered to be the national dish of Switzerland.

Zürcher Geschnetzeltes: Originally from Zurich, Zürcher Geschnetzeltes is a common menu item in Lucerne. It includes sliced veal that has been cooked in a smooth white wine and mushroom sauce and is paired with rösti. A great joy is the marriage of delicate meat and creamy sauce.

Lucerne's Food Markets and Culinary Delights

Lucerne's food markets must be visited to fully appreciate the city's gastronomic culture. Weekly farmers' markets, like the one at Helvetiaplatz, provide a wide selection of fresh fruit, artisanal goods, and local cheeses and meats. Talk to local merchants, try their wares, and collect supplies for a picnic or a home-cooked supper.

There are several gourmet stores and delicatessens in Lucerne where you can buy regional delicacies including Swiss chocolates, premium cheeses, cured meats, and local wines. Discover these businesses and have some Swiss cuisine.

You may choose from a wide variety of different cuisines in Lucerne, including Italian, French, Asian, and Mediterranean. There are several restaurants in the city, ranging from quaint pubs serving traditional Swiss food to expensive eateries providing cutting-edge culinary experiences. Make sure to try a range of foods and investigate the fusion of tastes available in Lucerne's eating scene.

Chocolate and Cheese Tastings: Indulge in Swiss Delicacies

Without indulging in some of Switzerland's world-famous cheeses and chocolates, a trip there would not be complete. There are many chances in Lucerne to sample and learn about these Swiss specialties:

Chocolate tastings: Indulge in a chocolate-tasting experience by visiting one of the numerous chocolate shops in Lucerne, such as Max Chocolatier or

Aeschbach Chocolatier. Discover the skill of chocolate production, indulge in a range of tastes and textures, and admire the artistry of these delicious delights.

Cheese tastings: Attend a cheese tasting session at a local dairy farm or cheese store. Various Swiss cheeses, such as Gruyère, Emmental, and Appenzeller, are sampled. Discover the many tastes, textures, and manufacturing processes that have made Swiss cheese so known across the globe.

Explore the food markets and gourmet stores in Lucerne, indulge in chocolate and cheese tastings, and learn about the rich tastes and skilled workmanship that go into these Swiss delicacies. Savor classic Swiss cuisines like fondue and rösti. Every food connoisseur will find something to satiate their taste buds in Lucerne's culinary scene, which provides a fascinating mix of history and innovation.

Immerse yourself in Lucerne's culinary offerings, and let the tastes of Switzerland transport you on an unforgettable culinary adventure.

DAY TRIPS FROM LUCERNE

While Lucerne has a wide range of sights and things to do, the area around it is as fascinating and deserving of study. Several day trip alternatives from Lucerne enable you to see the varied beauties of Switzerland, from picturesque mountains to energetic towns. Listed below are a few suggested day trips:

Lucerne to Mount Rigi: A Scenic Journey

Mount Rigi, sometimes referred to as the "Queen of Mountains," is a well-liked day trip destination and is just a short distance from Lucerne. Take a boat from Lucerne to Vitznau to start your tour, soaking in the beautiful scenery of Lake Lucerne as you go. Take the oldest cogwheel train in Europe, which departs from Vitznau, to reach Mount Rigi's peak.

Enjoy the spectacular views of the nearby Alps, lakes, and woods as you climb. Take a leisurely trek up the well-defined pathways until you reach the summit, or just sit back and take in the breathtaking views. In addition, Mount Rigi has a variety of restaurants where you may enjoy Swiss cuisine while taking in the natural splendor of the mountains.

Lucerne to Zurich: Exploring Switzerland's Largest City

A day excursion to Zurich, the biggest city in Switzerland, provides a contrast between the historical allure of Lucerne and the energetic metropolitan vibe of Zurich. Take the hour-long train ride to Zurich and start your city exploring from there.

Take a stroll along the Bahnhofstrasse, one of the most exclusive shopping alleys in the world, which is dotted with exquisite boutiques and landmark shops. Discover the Old Town's (Altstadt) surviving medieval structures, churches, and winding lanes. Visit historical sites including the Grossmünster, Fraumünster, and the Kunsthaus Zurich, which has a noteworthy collection of contemporary art.

Don't pass up the chance to take in Lake Zurich's bustling environment. Ride a boat, unwind by the water's edge, or have a delectable dinner at a waterfront restaurant. You may enjoy the culinary pleasures of Zurich by choosing from a wide variety of foreign cuisines and regional specialties.

Lucerne to Bern: The Capital's Charms

The Swiss capital city of Bern offers a fascinating alternative for a day excursion from Lucerne. By using the train, you can reach this attractive city with its well-preserved medieval old town—designated as a UNESCO World Heritage Site—in around 1.5 hours.

Wander the cobblestoned streets and discover Bern's historical sites, including the Zytglogge (Clock Tower), Bern Cathedral, and Bear Park, which is home to the bear that serves as Bern's emblem. Visit institutions like the Bern Historical Museum and the Museum of Communication to learn more about the city's rich history and cultural heritage.

Bern is recognized for its bustling culinary scene and active café culture. Take a stop at a "Konditorei," a kind of classic Swiss café, and savor some Swiss pastries and sweets. Don't forget to try Berner Platte, a substantial meal made up of a variety of meats, sausages, and conventional side dishes, which is a specialty of the area.

Lucerne to Interlaken: A Gateway to the Swiss Alps

A day excursion from Lucerne to Interlaken is strongly advised for people seeking beautiful alpine landscapes and outdoor experiences. The charming town of Interlaken is located between the two magnificent lakes of Lake Thun and Lake Brienz and is encircled by snow-capped mountains.

Train travel to Interlaken will provide you access to a variety of sites and activities. Take an exhilarating cable car journey to Harder Kulm's top for sweeping views of the Jungfrau area. Adventures in the great outdoors include hiking, paragliding, and river rafting. Discover the quaint town center, peruse the Swiss watch and gift stores, or relax by the lake and take in the gorgeous surroundings.

The famous Jungfrau area and the Swiss Alps can both be reached from Interlaken. If you have the time, think about extending your day trip so you may explore more. For example, you might take a cogwheel train to Jungfraujoch, sometimes known as the "Top of Europe," where you'll be rewarded with breathtaking vistas of glaciers and high peaks.

You'll have vivid recollections of Switzerland's breathtaking natural beauty and rich cultural heritage as you travel back to Lucerne after the day.

A great way to see the variety of Switzerland's landscapes, towns, and cultural sites is via day excursions from Lucerne. Each day excursion offers a distinctive experience that compliments your vacation to Lucerne, whether you decide to discover the breathtaking splendor of Mount Rigi, savor the lively energy of Zurich, dig into the historical allure of Bern, or delight in the alpine marvels of Interlaken.

FESTIVALS AND EVENTS IN LUCERNE

Lucerne Festival: A Celebration of Classical Music

The Lucerne Festival is an annual festival of classical music that is well-known across the world and takes place in the beautiful city of Lucerne, Switzerland. The festival, which was founded in 1938, has made a name for itself as one of the most prestigious classical music gatherings in the world, drawing world-famous orchestras, conductors, soloists, and chamber performers.

History and Prestige:
The Lucerne Festival has a distinguished past and a sterling reputation. Some of the finest artists and groups in the world have performed there throughout the years, including Herbert von Karajan, Claudio

Abbado, Sir Simon Rattle, Martha Argerich, and many more. The festival has established itself as one of the most famous music festivals in the world because of its dedication to musical excellence and innovation.

Venue:

The KKL Luzern (Lucerne Culture and Congress Center), the venerable Lucerne Concert Hall, and the beautiful outdoor site known as the Lucerne Festival Ark Nova are just a few of the famous locations where the festival is held across Lucerne. The whole musical experience is improved by the excellent acoustics and intriguing locations of these venues.

Concert schedule:

The Lucerne Festival presents a varied program that spans a variety of musical genres, from operas, vocal performances, and contemporary music to symphony concerts and chamber music recitals. The festival's program includes everything from classical classics to the world premieres of brand-new works, guaranteeing that spectators will have a rich and diverse musical experience.

Instrumental Residencies:

Reputable orchestras are welcomed as artists in residence at the event every year. Through a series of performances and collaborations with top conductors and performers, these residencies provide the orchestras the chance to highlight their sound and character. The festival's premier group, the Lucerne Festival Orchestra, is made up of outstanding artists from all around the globe.

Ateliers and Masterclasses:

Additionally, the Lucerne Festival provides educational opportunities including master classes and seminars offered by renowned artists. These changes provide ambitious young musicians the chance to learn from and be inspired by seasoned experts, encouraging musical development and identifying the next wave of talent.

Festival College:

Young instrumentalists, conductors, and composers may collaborate closely with accomplished mentors via the Lucerne Festival Academy, which was founded by famous composer and conductor Pierre Boulez. The culmination of the participants' intense preparations, performances, and educational endeavors are concerts that highlight their abilities.

Ambiance and atmosphere:

The event draws music fans from all backgrounds because of its lively and welcoming environment. The event is situated against the enchanting background of Lucerne, a lovely city with a rich history. The festival's surroundings provide visitors the opportunity to take in the cultural environment, attend pre-concert discussions, and take in the friendly vibe.

With its outstanding performances, a varied schedule, and continuous dedication to artistic quality, the Lucerne Festival is a celebration of classical music that mesmerizes audiences. The festival gives a fantastic chance to appreciate the beauty and force of music in the heart of Switzerland, whether you are an experienced classical music fan or a novice to the genre.

Fasnacht Lucerne: Carnival Extravaganza

The Lucerne Carnival, also known as Fasnacht Lucerne, is an annual carnival festival that takes place in the Swiss city of Lucerne. This annual celebration draws thousands of tourists from near and far, making it one of the biggest and most important carnivals in the nation. Lucerne's

Fasnacht is a time of jubilant festivity, vibrant costumes, upbeat music, and a festive ambiance. Let's look at some of this carnival extravaganza's highlights:

Tradition and History:
The origins of Fasnacht Luzern go back many centuries. The carnival's beginnings may be found in medieval times when it functioned as a celebration of the impending spring and a bid goodbye to winter. It has grown over time into a lavish spectacle that highlights Lucerne's rich cultural history.

Carnival parades:
In the early morning hours, when the city's lights are turned out and the streets are lit only by the gentle glow of lanterns carried by the participants, the carnival begins with a large procession known as the "Morgenstreich." The parade is a captivating show of color, music, and creativity that includes magnificent floats, costumed

figures, marching bands, and traditional masks.

Guggenmusik:

The vivacious Guggenmusik is a notable Fasnacht Lucerne feature. Brass and percussion-based Guggenmusik ensembles perform in public spaces like squares and pubs, infusing the air with upbeat and sometimes hilarious music. The contagious rhythms and melodies of Guggenmusik provide a joyful mood, and onlookers are invited to participate in the celebration by singing, dancing, and generally having a good time.

Masks and costumes:

Participants dress up for Fasnacht Lucerne in ornate and creative costumes that often represent regional folklore, historical personalities, or modern ideas. Masks are often used, and elaborately made masks give the carnival a sense of mystery and intrigue. These masks, which frequently have symbolic implications, depict a variety of figures from Swiss folklore and mythology.

Narren Spiegel:

The "Narrenspiegel" (Fool's Mirror) is another aspect of Fasnacht Lucerne that stands out. In this satirical tradition, political personalities, celebrities, and social concerns are portrayed in big, humorous caricatures. These amusing performances provide a lighter reflection on the news and give the carnival celebrations a dash of sarcasm.

Carnival for kids:

Family-friendly festivities like Fasnacht Lucerne have a Children's Carnival that welcomes children to participate in the festivities. Children enjoy unique activities and performances created especially for them, dress up in costumes, and take part in parades. By doing this, the essence of the carnival is preserved for future generations.

Balls and Events for Fasnacht:
Numerous balls and events are held during the carnival season, providing chances for dancing, live music performances, and mingling. These gatherings provide an opportunity to take part in the Fasnacht Lucerne celebrations in a more formal atmosphere.

Fasnacht Lucerne is an enthralling carnival spectacular that, with its fervor, inventiveness, and feeling of community, brings the city to life. Locals and tourists may both embrace the spirit of celebration during the carnival, let go of inhibitions, and take in the festive environment. Tradition, music, and the vivacious spirit of Lucerne come together at this time to provide a memorable experience for everyone who takes part.

Blue Balls Festival: Music and Arts on the Lake

An annual music and arts event called the Blue Balls event takes place in the charming Swiss city of Lucerne. The festival provides a unique and enthralling experience that mixes live music performances, visual arts, and a bustling environment thanks to its gorgeous setting on the beaches of Lake Lucerne. Let's look at the main features of this fascinating event:

Music Performances:

Rock, pop, jazz, blues, soul, and world music are among the many musical genres represented in the Blue Balls Festival's remarkable and eclectic list of performers. Both well-known acts and up-and-coming performers from Switzerland and other countries are included at the event. Concerts are held in a variety of indoor and outdoor locations that provide a variety of ambiances to suit various musical preferences.

Lake Stage:

The Lake Stage, a stunning outdoor location located on the shore of Lake Lucerne, is one of the festival's key draws. The festival-goers may enjoy the music while taking in the expansive views of the lake and the surrounding mountains thanks to this special location, which offers a breath-inspiring background for performances. A wonderfully magnificent atmosphere is produced by the blending of music, the natural world, and the sparkling waterways.

Visual Arts and Exhibitions:

The Blue Balls Festival offers a carefully organized schedule of visual arts and exhibits in addition to music. In addition to the musical performances, visitors may check out a range of art installations, photographic exhibitions, and multimedia displays. These creative components provide the event depth and innovation while giving visitors a multi-sensory experience.

Club Venues:
Several club locations in the city are offering smaller performances by up-and-coming musicians and bands as part of the festival, which extends beyond the Lake Stage. These smaller venues provide an intimate ambiance that enables music fans to discover fresh talent and enjoy the thrill of live music in a private setting.

Street Parade and Open-Air Events:
The Blue Balls Festival does not just take place in enclosed spaces. Throughout the festival, there are street parades, outdoor activities, and spontaneous performances that liven up the city's streets with music, dancing, and vivacious energy. Everyone has the opportunity to participate in these free outdoor activities and take in the vibrant ambiance while getting a taste of the festival's spirit.

Food and Drink:

No celebration would be complete without delectable food and hydrating drinks. The Blue Balls Festival offers a selection of food booths and bars where attendees may enjoy regional Swiss cuisine, foreign cuisine, and specialty beverages. Every appetite may be satiated with a variety of savory and sweet delicacies.

Late Night Sessions:
The Blue Balls Festival offers late-night performances that go on into the wee hours of the morning for anyone wanting a nocturnal musical experience. For night owls and music lovers, these events often include experimental and cutting-edge music, offering a distinctive and immersive experience.

With Lake Lucerne as its stunning background, the Blue Balls Festival is a celebration of music, art, and culture. It provides a platform for both well-known and up-and-coming artists, encouraging creativity and creating a special experience for everyone who attends. The Blue Balls Festival is a must-attend event whether you like music, and art, or are just looking for a fun and energetic environment.

Lucerne Christmas Market: Magical Holiday Spirit

During the holiday season, the heart of Switzerland's Lucerne hosts the lovely and spectacular Lucerne Christmas Market. The Christmas Market, which is popular for its gorgeous location and merry vibe, attracts both residents and tourists who want to take in the wonder and pleasure of the holiday season. Let's examine the main features of this great occasion:

Location and Setting:
The Old Town, where the Lucerne Christmas Market is housed, provides a picturesque and idyllic setting for the celebrations. The atmosphere is reminiscent

of a fairy tale thanks to the old buildings, winding cobblestone streets, and dazzling lights.

Holiday Markets and Shopping:
The market is made up of various booths, each of which sells a range of one-of-a-kind items. Visitors may browse a variety of regionally prepared food and drinks, seasonal decorations, handcrafted gifts, and traditional crafts. The market offers a wide variety of chances for Christmas shopping and discovering unique items, from expertly carved wooden decorations to fragrant spices and snacks.

Christmas Illuminations:
As the sun sets, the Christmas Market is exquisitely decorated with holiday lighting, which creates a lovely ambiance. The market is filled with a warm, welcoming glow and a hint of glitter thanks to the lights, which further heighten the festive mood.

Culinary delights:

The variety of delectable foods on sale at the Lucerne Christmas Market is one of its attractions. There are many foods to savor and warm the spirit throughout the winter, from sizzling sausages and roasted chestnuts to gingerbread cookies and hot mulled wine. The air is filled with the enticing fragrances of both traditional Swiss food and other cuisines from across the world.

Live Music and Entertainment:

The Christmas Market offers live musical performances, choirs, and cultural displays to heighten the holiday spirit. Christmas carols, live music, and traditional Swiss music are all available for visitors to take in, making for a joyous and uplifting experience for everyone.

Ice Skating:

The ice skating rink at the Lucerne Christmas Market is a well-liked feature.

The skating rink, which is situated in the main area, offers both novice and expert skaters a distinctive and enjoyable experience. While taking in the sights and sounds of the market, visitors may glide over the ice and make unforgettable moments with their loved ones.

Santa Claus and Children's Activities:
With a variety of events and attractions to keep them busy, the market is a sanctuary for kids. Small presents and the opportunity to communicate their desires with Santa Claus are available for children. Additionally, there are engaging workshops, storytelling events, and enjoyable rides to keep children entertained and caught up in the holiday spirit.

The festive spirit and charm are captured by the Lucerne Christmas Market. It fosters a feeling of warmth and community by bringing people together to enjoy the spirit of Christmas with its festive booths, sparkling lights, culinary delights, live music, and an upbeat environment. The Lucerne Christmas Market is a must-go location that will leave you with enduring memories of a genuinely magical experience, whether you're looking for one-of-a-kind presents, delectable sweets, or just a dose of seasonal happiness.

PRACTICAL INFORMATION FOR TRAVELERS

Accommodation Options: Hotels, Hostels, and More

Numerous lodging choices are available in Lucerne to accommodate various tastes and price ranges. You'll discover a variety of options to guarantee a comfortable and memorable stay, whether you're seeking luxury hotels, quaint boutique lodgings, budget-friendly hostels, or vacation rentals. Let's look at some of the lodging possibilities in Lucerne:

1. **Hotels:**
Several hotels in Lucerne can accommodate different wants and requirements. Hotels

provide a variety of facilities and services to improve your stay, from opulent five-star places to cozy midrange alternatives. Many of the hotels in Lucerne have breathtaking views of the lake or the mountains in the area, and others are housed in old structures, which adds to the beauty of your stay.

2. **Boutique Hotels:**

Consider booking a room at one of Lucerne's boutique hotels for a more distinctive and individualized experience. These more intimate, sometimes privately-owned accommodations provide tastefully decorated rooms, careful service, and a homey ambiance. The distinctive nature of Lucerne's boutique hotels makes them the perfect choice for tourists looking for a more personal and genuine lodging experience.

3. **Hostels:**

Lucerne features several hostels that provide inexpensive lodging alternatives whether you're a frugal tourist or want a more sociable setting. Hostels provide private rooms for people who want more privacy in addition to dormitory-style dormitories with common bathrooms. They are an excellent option for lone travelers, backpackers, and people trying to meet other travelers since they often offer common spaces, shared kitchens, and planned activities.

4. **Vacation Rentals and Apartments:**

Vacation rentals and apartments in Lucerne are a popular option for individuals who desire greater room and the comfort of a homelike atmosphere. These choices include anything from completely furnished apartments to vacation houses and villas. Vacation rentals provide you the freedom to make your meals, take advantage of extra living space, and discover a place like a resident.

5. **Bed and Breakfasts:**

Another choice to take into consideration is bed and breakfast lodgings. Many quaint B&Bs in Lucerne provide cozy accommodations, a sumptuous breakfast, and attentive service. These places often feature a warm, inviting environment that seems like a home away from home.

6. **Lakefront Accommodations:**
Consider lodging on Lake Lucerne's beaches for a very gorgeous stay. Many hotels and guesthouses provide easy access to the lake, breathtaking views, and the chance to engage in leisure activities like swimming, boating, or lakeside strolls just outside your door.

7. **Wellness and Spa Resorts:**
If pampering and relaxation are top of your list of priorities, Lucerne features health and spa resorts that provide a variety of reviving treatments, wellness amenities, and peaceful settings. These resorts provide a haven for relaxation as well as an

all-encompassing experience centered on wellness.

Think about things like location, facilities, cost, and the experience you want while selecting lodging in Lucerne. It is essential to make reservations in advance, particularly during busy times, to lock in your first option and guarantee a smooth and comfortable stay in this beautiful Swiss city.

Transportation within Lucerne: Buses, Trains, and Boats

The fast and convenient public transit system in Lucerne makes getting around easy. There are several ways to get about Lucerne and its surroundings, whether you like buses, trains, or boats. Following is a list of Lucerne's many transportation options:

1. **Buses:**

In Lucerne, there is a robust local bus system that serves both the city and the surrounding areas. Buses are a practical method to get to Lucerne, giving you access to the city's well-known sights, neighborhoods, and transit hubs. The buses are spotless, comfy, and furnished with extras like voice announcements and real-time information screens. At significant bus stops, ticket vending machines are available for purchase as well as abroad.

2. **Trains:**

Train travel is a convenient method to move to Lucerne and see other parts of Switzerland since the city is well-connected to the Swiss rail network. Lucerne's main railway station, Lucerne Bahnhof, is a significant transportation hub that provides links to several local and distant locations. Switzerland's trains are renowned for their timeliness, comfort, and picturesque itineraries, making for a pleasurable journey.

3. **Lake Lucerne Boats:**

Known also as Lake Vierwaldstättersee, Lake Lucerne is not only a beautiful tourist destination but also a means of transit. A fleet of passenger boats that link the numerous towns and villages along the lake's shores and provide picturesque trips serves the area. You can reach places like Weggis, Vitznau, and Beckenried with ease by taking a boat trip on Lake Lucerne, which offers breathtaking views of the Alps nearby. Regular boat service is provided, particularly during the tourist season.

4. **Walking and Bicycling:**

Lucerne is a city that encourages pedestrians, and many of its attractions are close to one another. The city's well-kept sidewalks and designated pedestrian areas make it simple to stroll about on foot. Those who like riding bicycles have designated cycling pathways in Lucerne as well. A pleasant and eco-friendly option to see

Lucerne and its surroundings is to hire a bicycle from one of the city's many rental shops.

5. **Car Rental and Taxis:**
Even though using public transit is quick and easy, some tourists may prefer the adaptability and convenience of using a cab or renting a vehicle. The Lucerne railway station and various places in the city provide car rental services. You may also call a cab or reserve one in advance for a private trip.

It is advised to verify the timetables and map out your route before exploring Lucerne. The Swiss Travel Pass, a well-liked choice for tourists, offers unlimited public transit use over a certain period and includes discounts at attractions. The Lucerne public transportation website and the ticket booths at the railway station both include details on routes, timetables, and ticket costs.

The city of Lucerne and its surroundings are easily explored thanks to its effective public transit system. You'll have easy access to the city's attractions, natural beauty, and nearby areas whether you choose buses, trains, boats, or a mix of these modes, assuring a smooth and delightful travel experience.

Important Travel Advice and Safety Advice

To guarantee a smooth and pleasurable journey, it's necessary to bear in mind some crucial travel advice and safety information while visiting Lucerne, Switzerland. Here are some important things to think about:

1. **Travel Documents:**
Make sure your passport is up to date and has at least six more months before the day you want to travel. Before visiting Switzerland, you may need to apply for a visa, depending on your nationality. Ahead

of time, research the visa requirements and apply if required.

2. **Safety and Health:**

The healthcare system of Switzerland, particularly Lucerne, is first-rate. It is advised to get travel insurance that includes emergency medical evacuation coverage for medical costs. Keep a copy of your prescriptions with you at all times, and bring any essential drugs. Drinking Lucerne's tap water is safe.

3. **Climate and Clothes:**

Depending on the season, the weather in Lucerne might change. Layers of clothes are recommended since temperatures might fluctuate throughout the day. Bring a waterproof jacket if you want to engage in outdoor activities or travel at a time of heavy precipitation.

4. **Payments and Currency:**

The Swiss Franc (CHF) is the nation of Switzerland's official currency. Although most businesses take credit cards, it's always a good idea to have some cash on hand for little purchases and transactions. There are several ATMs scattered across the city.

5. **Mobility and Getting Around:**

Buses, trains, and boats are all part of the efficient public transit system in Lucerne, as was already noted. For unlimited travel and reduced entrance to attractions, think about buying a Swiss Travel Pass or other regional passes. Plan your trips following the transit timetables that you are familiar with.

6. **Local traditions and manners:**

Switzerland has its unique traditions and manners. When entering a store or restaurant, it's usual to shake hands and say "Guten Tag" (Good day). Tipping is encouraged but not required. For excellent service, it's customary to round up the amount or provide a tiny gratuity.

7. **Considering the Environment:**

Because of Switzerland's unspoiled natural beauty, it's important to practice environmental sensitivity. When hiking, stick to the established routes, dispose of rubbish properly, and heed any warnings or instructions on the preservation of the natural environment.

8. **Security and Safety:**

Although Lucerne is usually regarded as a secure city, it is always a good idea to be cautious. Watch your valuables and be on the lookout for pickpockets, particularly in busy places. When visiting new places, use caution and avoid going on a late-night stroll alone.

9. **Emergency numbers:**

Save emergency phone numbers, such as those for the neighborhood police (117) and medical services (144), to your phone, and get to know the closest hospitals and medical facilities.

Keep track of any travel advice or regulations released by the government of your home country regarding visits to Switzerland.

You may have a great and stress-free time while seeing the lovely city of Lucerne by paying attention to this travel advice and emphasizing your safety.

Shopping in Lucerne: Souvenirs and Local Products

Shopping in Lucerne is a joy, with many choices for finding distinctive gifts, regional goods, and Swiss delicacies. Whether you're seeking mouth watering chocolates, classic Swiss crafts, or fine watches, Lucerne offers something to satisfy every taste. Here are some highlights and suggestions for shopping:

Swiss Watches and Jewelry:

Lucerne is a great spot to purchase top-notch Swiss timepieces since Switzerland is known for its accuracy and workmanship in watchmaking. Visit watch stores and boutiques in the city center to browse a variety of watches, from pricey selections to premium names. Additionally, you may get magnificent jewelry that was manufactured in Switzerland, complete with elaborate patterns and themes.

Swiss confectionery & chocolates:

Visit the Lucerne chocolate boutiques to indulge in the world-famous Swiss chocolates. A delicious selection of handmade Swiss chocolates, truffles, pralines, and other confections are available from companies including Läderach, Sprüngli, and Max Chocolatier. These stores make it easy to taste and choose from a wide range of flavors and packaging choices, making them ideal for giving or treating yourself.

Swiss cheese with regional cuisine:

Swiss cheese and other local delicacies may be found and explored in Lucerne. You may try and buy a range of Swiss cheeses, such as Gruyère, Emmental, Appenzeller, and more, at nearby cheese stores like Chäslade and Swiss Cheese Corner. Additionally, you may discover typical Swiss foods like honey, preserves, honey, and chocolate spreads. These delectable treats may be added to your cupboard or make wonderful presents.

Swiss Crafts and Souvenirs:

In the Old Town of Lucerne, you may find classic Swiss trinkets and crafts. Discover stores that specialize in selling items manufactured in Switzerland, like dirndls, lederhosen, cowbells, music boxes, needlework, and wooden sculptures. These objects are distinctive and unforgettable keepsakes that showcase Switzerland's rich cultural history.

Knives & Cutlery from Switzerland:

Swiss Army knives are renowned for their adaptability and accuracy and are classic Swiss items. Lucerne is home to shops selling Swiss Army knives in a variety of styles, sizes, and accessories. You might also look at Swiss cookware and cutlery, which are renowned for their superb quality and workmanship.

Gallery of Arts and Crafts:

You may find locally produced artwork, pottery, glassware, and sculptures at Lucerne's many art galleries and craft stores. These galleries often feature the creations of Swiss artists and craftspeople, giving patrons the chance to take home a one-of-a-kind item of Swiss art.

Street Markets and Farmers' Markets:

You may be able to attend the street markets and farmers' markets in Lucerne if you go there at the proper time of year. A variety of homemade handicrafts, regional vegetables, and seasonal goods are available at the Christmas market during the holiday season and in sporadic street markets year-round.

Remember the tourist value-added tax (VAT) rebate program when you buy in Lucerne. If you fulfill the requirements, you may request a refund of the VAT you paid on qualifying purchases when you leave Switzerland. Look for retailers with the "Tax-Free Shopping" badge, and ask how the procedure works while making a purchase.

Enjoy the Lucerne shopping experience as you peruse the varied selection of Swiss watches, chocolates, mementos, and regional goods. Bring a bit of Switzerland's rich cultural history home while indulging in the fine workmanship and delectable tastes that make Swiss goods so unique.

Lucerne Travel Itineraries

Here are two recommended journeys for discovering Lucerne and its surroundings:

Option 1: Highlights of Lucerne (2–3 Days)

Day 1:

Morning: Visit Lucerne's Old Town to kick off your day. Visit the nearby Water Tower and the famous Chapel Bridge (Kapellbrücke), one of Switzerland's oldest covered wooden bridges. Take a walk around the lovely streets and take in the gorgeous scenery and old-world architecture.

Afternoon: Visit the Swiss Museum of Transport in the afternoon, which is outside the city limits. With the help of interactive exhibitions, antique cars, and simulators, you can completely immerse yourself in the fascinating world of transportation history and technology.

Evening: Savor Swiss delicacies and stunning views of Lake Lucerne while having a leisurely meal at one of the lakefront restaurants.

Day 2:

Morning: Early in the morning, take a lake cruise to see the area's scenery. You may trek or ride a cable car to the peak of Mount Rigi or Mount Pilatus, where you can also enjoy stunning views.

Afternoon: The Lion Monument (Löwendenkmal), a striking monument carved into a rock face in honor of the Swiss Guards who sacrificed their lives during the French Revolution, may be seen in the afternoon when you return to Lucerne.

Evening: Take in Lucerne's thriving dining scene by choosing between local fare at a classic Swiss restaurant or an international menu at one of the city's numerous restaurants.

Optional Day 3 :

If you have spare time, think about visiting Engelberg-Titlis for the day. Take part in alpine activities like skiing, snowboarding, or hiking, and ride a cable car to Mount Titlis' summit for sweeping vistas of the Swiss Alps.

Option 2: Lucerne and the Beauty of the Region (4-5 Days)

Day 1:

Morning: Tour the Old Town of Lucerne, taking in its Chapel Bridge, Water Tower, and Musegg Wall. A tower along the city walls may be climbed for a bird's-eye perspective of Lucerne.

Afternoon: Visit the Richard Wagner Museum in the afternoon, which is close to Lake Lucerne. Through exhibitions and multimedia presentations, learn about the famous composer's life and creative output.

Evening: Savor a leisurely supper at a lakeside restaurant while taking in the serene lake views and delecting on Swiss cuisine.

Day 2:

Morning: Take a boat journey to Weggis, a beautiful village dubbed the "Riviera of Lake Lucerne," and explore its quaint streets and cable car station before ascending to Mount Rigi for breathtaking views.

Afternoon: Travel back to Lucerne and explore the history of Swiss transportation at the Swiss Museum of Transport.

Evening: Take in the tranquil ambiance in one of Lucerne's numerous lakeside parks or gardens.

Day 3:

Morning: Early in the morning, go for a day excursion to Zurich. Visit the Grossmünster und Fraumünster, take a walk along the bustling Bahnhofstrasse, and explore the ancient Old Town.

Afternoon: Examine the Kunsthaus Zurich in the afternoon, which is renowned for its magnificent collection of modern and contemporary art.

Evening: Travel back to Lucerne and have dinner at a quaint restaurant where you may sample Swiss delicacies or other cuisines.

Day 4:

Morning: Visit the quaint village of Engelberg in the morning. Spend time outside snowboarding, skiing, or hiking after riding a cable car up Mount Titlis for beautiful vistas.

Afternoon: Take a tour of Engelberg Abbey, a Benedictine abbey with a fascinating past and stunning construction.

Evening: Unwind and take in Engelberg's inviting ambiance while possibly indulging in a sumptuous Swiss fondue meal.

These itineraries provide a place to start discovering Lucerne and its surroundings. You are free to alter them following your tastes and the amount of time you have. There are many things to do and see in Lucerne, which makes for a wonderful trip to this lovely Swiss city.

CONCLUSION

Final Thoughts on Lucerne

Visitors are enthralled by Lucerne's alluring beauty, extensive history, and energetic environment. The city provides the ideal fusion of natural marvels and cultural pleasures as it is tucked away between breathtaking mountainous vistas and Lake Lucerne. Every aspect of Lucerne, from the recognizable Chapel Bridge and the charming Old Town to the tranquil lakeside promenades, emanates a certain charm that makes an impact on everyone who visits.

The Old Town of Lucerne is a veritable treasure trove of history and culture with its well-preserved medieval buildings, cobblestone lanes, and charming squares. You may find quaint boutiques, pleasant cafés, and a variety of undiscovered jewels by exploring the little lanes.

With the glistening Lake Lucerne and the Reuss River winding through its center, the city's ties to the water are clear. The lake offers chances for leisurely boat excursions, lakeside strolls, and water activities in addition to its beautiful vistas.

Lucerne is recognized for its dedication to the arts and has a lively cultural and music scene. Visitors may immerse themselves in a world of classical music, modern art, and dramatic productions, from the renowned Lucerne Festival to the countless galleries and museums.

The city's accessibility is one of its best features. The majestic Swiss Alps may be accessed from Lucerne through a short drive to summits like Mount Pilatus and Mount Rigi. There are several outdoor activities available, ranging from paragliding and mountain biking to hiking and skiing.

The lively Fasnacht Lucerne carnival and the enchanted Christmas market are just two of the many festivals and events that Lucerne offers all year long to enhance the city's appeal and foster a feeling of celebration and community.

You may sample Swiss cheese and chocolate in Lucerne, as well as experience the kind hospitality of the Swiss, in addition to enjoying the delicacies of Swiss food.

Whether you're looking for scenic natural beauty, cultural activities, outdoor adventures, or just a peaceful break from daily life, Lucerne is a location that appeals to all sorts of people. A genuinely remarkable experience is guaranteed by the region's blend of breathtaking vistas, extensive history, and energetic environment.

Allow yourself to be mesmerized by Lucerne's timeless beauty, immerse yourself in its fascinating history, and savor the welcoming atmosphere that makes this Swiss city such a special place to visit while you wander about.

Planning Your Perfect Trip to Lucerne

It may be thrilling and rewarding to plan your vacation to Lucerne. Here are some ideas to keep in mind when you plan your ideal itinerary:

Establish the length of your trip:
Choose the length of your stay in Lucerne. Think about the things you want to do, your budget, and the time you have available for vacation. While Lucerne may be thoroughly explored in a few days, staying longer, if possible, offers a more leisurely and immersive experience.

Find the Ideal Time to Visit:

When selecting your vacation dates, consider the weather and seasonal attractions. The summer months (June to August), when the weather is often warm and pleasant, are Lucerne's busiest travel times. There are fewer people and warmer temperatures in the spring (April to May) and fall (September to October). A lovely time to go is during the winter (December to February) when there are opportunities for snow sports and Christmas markets.

Choose Your Interests:

To customize your itinerary, take into account your tastes and interests. Are you more interested in outdoor activities, gastronomic experiences, or history and culture? Determine your goals and concentrate on those areas throughout your vacation to Lucerne, which provides a varied choice of activities to satisfy different interests.

Create a List of Must-See Attractions:
Make a list of the top attractions in Lucerne that you can't miss after doing some research on them. Landmarks like the Chapel Bridge, the Lion Monument, the Old Town, and the Swiss Museum of Transport may be included in this list. When planning your schedule, take into account any particular occasions or festivals that coincide with the dates of your trip.

Plan Day Trips:
The central position of Lucerne gives it a great starting point for day visits to adjacent places. Make time in your schedule for visits to local sights like Zurich, Engelberg, Mount Rigi, and Mount Pilatus after doing some research on them. To guarantee a smooth day trip, arrange transportation and verify the timetables for any boats, trains, or buses.

Balance Your Itinerary:

For exploration and relaxation, strike a balance between planned activities and free time. While having a plan is essential, you should also allow for spontaneity and the possibility of making unexpected discoveries while exploring Lucerne's attractive streets and districts.

Accommodation and Transportation:

To guarantee your favorite option, do your research and make your reservations early. Budget, facilities, and location are important considerations. Choose the most practical means of transportation for your plan, whether it's taking the bus, renting a vehicle, or doing both at once.

Consider Local Experiences:

Discover new activities to fully immerse oneself in the culture of the area. This can be going to a classical music concert, trying Swiss food at nearby eateries, or taking part in a traditional Swiss cheese or chocolate tasting.

Consult travel advice and regulations:
Keep track of any travel warnings or recommendations issued by the Swiss authorities and the government of your home country before your trip. Make sure you have the proper travel documentation, including a passport that is up to date and any necessary visas.

Pack appropriately:
According to the season and the activities you want to participate in, pack the necessary clothes and items. Remember to pack any required devices or adapters, along with a pair of suitable walking shoes and clothing for the changeable weather.

When designing the ideal vacation to Lucerne, keep in mind that flexibility is crucial. Be prepared to make changes along the road to account for unanticipated events or brand-new possibilities that emerge. Accept Lucerne's beauty and allure, and take pleasure in the adventure as you discover this magnificent Swiss city.

Useful Resources and Contacts

There are several helpful connections and services you may utilize to arrange your trip to Lucerne and get helpful advice. Here are some important sources to think about:

Lucerne Tourism Office:

- For information about the city of Lucerne, see the official Lucerne Tourism Office. They provide leaflets, maps, and instructions on attractions, activities, lodging, transportation, and other topics. For individualized help, you may go to their website or get in touch with them.
- Website address: *luzern.com*
- Email: info@luzern.com.
- Phone: +41 41 227 17 17

Swiss Travel System:

- The Swiss Travel System provides several pass options that allow unrestricted use of all modes of public transportation in Switzerland, including trains, buses, and boats. When visiting Lucerne and other Swiss locations, the Swiss Travel Pass and regional passes should be taken into consideration.
- Website: ***www.swiss-pass.ch***

Public Transportation in Lucerne:
- Consult the official website of Verkehrsbetriebe Luzern (VBL), the city's public transportation provider, for details on bus, rail, and boat timetables, rates, and routes.
- Website: ***www.vbl.ch***

Swiss Federal Railways (SBB):
- The national railroad of Switzerland, the Swiss Federal Railways, offers extensive train services all around the nation. Timetables, ticket purchasing,

and details on train connections to and from Lucerne are all available on the SBB website and mobile app.

- Website: **www.sbb.ch**

Lucerne Weather Forecast:

- To organize your activities and bring the right gear for your vacation, check the Lucerne weather forecast. MeteoSwiss and Weather.com are only two examples of websites and mobile applications with trustworthy weather predictions.
- Website: ***www.meteoswiss.admin.ch, www.weather.com***

Consulate or Embassy:

- Find the closest embassy or consulate of your home country in Switzerland if you are visiting from another nation. They can help with emergencies, passport problems, and other consular services.

These connections and resources ought to guide you through your trip to Lucerne and provide you with the knowledge you need to have a simple and pleasurable time there. Do not be afraid to contact these groups if you have any special questions or need help while you are there.

Printed in Great Britain
by Amazon